N

SOCCER

BY CLIVE TOYE

A FIRST BOOK • REVISED EDITION
FRANKLIN WATTS • NEW YORK • LONDON • 1979

796.33
T

Cover photograph courtesy of Leo deWys.

Photographs courtesy of: United Press International: opp. p. 1, pp. 4 (top and bottom), 5 (bottom); FIFA, Zurich (Sculptor: Silvio Gazzaniga, Producer: Bertoni-Milano): p. 5 (top), Copyright FIFA; Bill Smith: pp. 11, 14, 18, 23, 28 (top and bottom), 34 (top and bottom), 38 (top and bottom), 42, 44, 47, 51.

Acknowledgment is made to these fine soccer players who are not iden-tified in the photo captions: Dick Advocaat, p. 42; Mervyn Cawston, p. 34 (top); Robert Gadocha, pp. 28 (top), 38 (top); Clive Griffiths, p. 23; Shep Messing, p. 34 (bottom); Gary Rensing, pp. 28 (bottom), 38 (bottom); Alex Skotarek, p. 44; Derek Spalding, pp. 6, 47.

Library of Congress Cataloging in Publication Data

Toye, Clive.
    Soccer.

(A First book)
Includes index.
SUMMARY: Introduces the world's fastest-growing and most popular sport, including its history and playing techniques.
1. Soccer — Juvenile literature. [1. Soccer] I. Title.
GV943.25.T69 1979   796.33′42   78-24314
ISBN 0-531-02936-0

CONTENTS

SOCCER

**More than 77,000 soccer fans watch the 1977
New York Cosmos — Fort Lauderdale Strikers
game at Giants Stadium in the Meadowlands,
East Rutherford, New Jersey.**

SOCCER—THE WORLD GAME

Someone somewhere in the world is playing soccer right now, for soccer is the one game that never sleeps. It is the one truly international sport.

Soccer may be played before 80,000 fans in Milan, Italy, or 120,000 in Lenin Stadium, Moscow; it may be watched by 100,000 Chinese in Peking or as many as 77,000 Americans in "Cosmos Country," the Meadowlands, in New Jersey.

The game is played on the equator, in Quito, Ecuador, and within the Arctic Circle, in Sweden — in hot or cold countries and far and wide over the globe. In fact, soccer is enjoyed in every nation on earth. And if ever a sporting event is held on the moon, there's a good chance the first game will be soccer.

Although the sport is called by a variety of names — *Fussball* in Germany, *futebol* in Brazil, *futbol* in Spain, *voetbal* in Holland, and *il calcio* in Italy —the official name of soccer is "association football." In England, where the game began long ago, people took the three letters s o c from "association" and turned them into the word "soccer."

To make sure that athletes in Paraguay play the same game as those in Hungary or Australia, the FIFA was formed in 1904.

This ruling body is formally known, in French, as the Fédération Internationale de Football Association, from which the initials FIFA are derived. In English, it is called the International Federation of Association Football. A total of 148 nations pay dues and accept the authority of FIFA.

FIFA controls the sport by issuing the playing rules of the game, known as the Laws of the Game, which are adhered to all over the world except for some minor and experimental variations.

For example, in an effort to increase scoring chances, the North American Soccer League has a smaller offside area than European countries have and has banished tie games by having teams play a sudden-death overtime period. Then, if the game is still tied, a dramatic one-on-one finale, called the NASL Shoot Out, takes place.

FIFA also organizes the massive World Cup competition every four years and acts as a clearing house for the movement of players from one country to another.

Although the United States Soccer Federation, affiliated with FIFA, was formed as early as 1913, the game was largely neglected in North America, and many playing rules were changed to suit local conditions. But the whole picture began to change in 1967 when the first coast-to-coast major professional soccer league was established in North America. Called the National Professional Soccer League, it had nine teams in the United States —and one team in Canada.

In the first championship play-offs, the Oakland Clippers beat the Baltimore Bays, and the attention of the soccer-playing world was focused for the first time on North America.

In 1968, the National Professional Soccer League merged

with the United Soccer Association — a rival league of imported foreign teams, which had also begun in 1967 — to form the North American Soccer League. Now North America had truly joined the world of soccer.

It seemed, for a time, as if those early efforts were going to end in failure, too. The NASL was reduced to only five teams in 1969. But gradually huge youth development plans were put into effect, and the game, as well as the NASL, grew and grew to major proportions by 1977.

The greatest increase in popularity began when Pele, regarded as the greatest player of all time, signed for the New York Cosmos. By the time Pele retired — in an emotional farewell in competition against his only previous club, Santos, on October 1, 1977 — the United States has had as many as 77,000 fans attending a single soccer game. And all over the country, crowds of 20,000 to 50,000 were occurring regularly.

At the same time, there was an even more dramatic growth in the number of youngsters playing soccer. In almost every community, youth leagues sprang up and began to produce outstanding young athletes for high school, college, and — eventually — pro soccer.

Although it is said that this multinational sport began in England about the eleventh century, historians have discovered that a form of soccer was played in China as long ago as 2000 B.C.

Several English kings banned the game because it was too dangerous and time-consuming. It kept their subjects from archery practice, the skill vitally needed at that time, because the bow and arrow were among the chief defensive weapons used in battle.

Opposite, top: in the 1978 World Cup game, Poland's Szamarch (left) and Peru's Cueto fight for control of the ball. Opposite, bottom: the incomparable Pele of the New York Cosmos dribbles past two Dallas Tornado players in a 1975 game. Right: the FIFA World Cup. Below: Mario Kempes of Argentina leaps in triumph after scoring a goal in the 1978 World Cup Final against Holland.

Organized soccer first appeared in England in 1863, when the English Football Association was formed as the governing body of the sport. Soccer was then played by amateur clubs and university teams, but by 1885 the game had become professional.

In the season of 1888–89, the original Football League was formed from the twelve strongest professional clubs. By the mid-twentieth century, the Football Association represented approximately 50,000 clubs in England. Some of its main functions include controlling and organizing international matches, and coaching and refereeing games. In 1901, a crowd of more than 100,000 paid to see the English Cup finals. To this day, the finals draw equally large numbers of fans every spring.

Gradually, the game spread — largely through British teams and British sailors or emigrants — to Europe and South America. Today, with the coming of major-league tournaments to the United States and Canada, soccer is truly the world's most popular sport.

THE WORLD CUP

The biggest and most important of the thousands of soccer competitions is the World Cup. This competition takes place in a different country every four years midway between the years of the Olympic Games. It is a great triumph for a soccer player to represent his country in the World Cup tournament and an even greater triumph if his team should make it to the finals. It takes two years of elimination play to reach the finals of the World Cup, where the best sixteen national teams fight it out.

The first World Cup winner was Uruguay, in 1930, followed by Italy, in 1934 and 1938. World War II stopped the competition, and it did not resume until 1950. Uruguay won again, beating Brazil before 200,000 stunned spectators in the biggest soccer stadium in the world — Maracana, in Rio de Janeiro. West Germany became the champion in 1954. Then Brazil took over the leadership in 1958 and 1962 with the help of Pele, probably the highest-paid athlete in the world. In 1966, England beat West Germany in extra time. The game was watched by a television audience estimated at more than 400,000,000.

That figure was exceeded in later World Cup finals — in 1970, when Brazil beat Italy in Mexico, and in 1974, when West Germany defeated Holland in Munich.

The world hailed a new World Cup champion in 1978, more than 1,000,000,000 people watching on TV around the world as Argentina, the host nation, beat Holland 3–1.

It was estimated that more than 6,000,000 people poured into the streets of Buenos Aires to celebrate their nation's success, in contrast to the gloom in Holland at their second defeat in the World Cup final in four years.

Back in 1974 Holland had been beaten 2–1 by West Germany, in regulation time. In 1978, the score was 1–1 after 90 minutes (with Holland hitting the goal post with what would have been the winner in the last 30 seconds of play) before Argentina triumphed in extra time.

Neither Argentina nor Holland had won the World Cup previously. Of the old champions, neither Uruguay nor England qualified for the final competition among 16 countries; West Germany went out after the second round; Italy finished fourth and Brazil had to be content with third place.

As a new champion emerged, so did another superstar — 23-year-old forward Mario Kempes, who scored two of Argentina's goals against Holland and finished as the tournament's leading goal scorer.

But even as Argentina was celebrating and the Dutch team flying sadly home, administrators, coaches and players around the world were beginning to prepare for the next test of world strength, the 1982 World Cup in Spain.

The World Cup was originally named the Jules Rimet Trophy, after the founder of FIFA, but that prize coveted by all the nations of the world now is called simply the FIFA World Cup.

All World Cup winning players receive huge bonuses, but some get special distinctions. For example, England's winning coach, Alf Ramsey, was knighted by Queen Elizabeth II after the 1966 win.

The United States has regularly competed in the World Cup but so far has usually been eliminated early in the competition. In 1930, however, when teams from many countries walked out at the last minute, the U.S. team finished third. And in 1950, although finishing well down the list, the United States startled all soccer fans by beating England, 1–0.

THE CLUBS

Each nation has its own soccer league championship. In Europe and South America, the champion club from each country goes on to compete for the European Cup or the South American Cup. The European and South American champions then meet for the World Club championship.

At the amateur level, the biggest competition is in the Olympic Games, which, like the World Cup contest, take place every four years. The teams compete for the honor of winning the gold, silver, or bronze award medals.

THE SPORT

Although soccer is called "football" in some countries, it is not at all like American football. It differs in that no soccer player except the goalkeeper may touch the ball with his hands. The ball must be kicked or "headed," that is, the head is used to bounce the ball away. And, unlike American football, soccer is a game of continuous action and individual initiative. About the only similarity is that in both games, two teams, each made up eleven players, oppose each other on the field of play.

Soccer is a team sport that demands high levels of skill, fitness, and effort. Yet it is a game that anyone can play and enjoy and does not require expensive equipment.

No particular physique is needed to play soccer. Height is not a factor, as it is in basketball; nor is weight, as in American football. In fact, many other sportsmen would be too big, too heavy, or too awkward to execute the maneuvers that a soccer player performs regularly.

However, good physical condition is a necessity in soccer. At the pro and other high levels of the game there is very little substitution, so each of the eleven players must go on the field prepared to play without rest for the entire game.

The game lasts for 90 minutes, and there is a half-time break of 10 to 15 minutes. When young boys and girls play the game, timing and the size of the field can be changed slightly to accommodate them, as long as the basic rules are kept. Indeed, because so many boys and girls now want to play the game, the rules on substitution are often relaxed to allow everyone on the team to play at least half a game.

THE EQUIPMENT

Soccer is an inexpensive game. The most important item of equipment is the shoes, or "boots." It is with these that a player must control the ball. (Only the goalkeeper may use his hands to touch the ball on the field of play.) A good soccer player controls the ball with his feet, or traps it with his thighs or chest, doing it as well as most people can by using their hands. Thus the player's boots must fit him so that he can feel the ball through them, and they must be comfortable enough to run around in for 90 minutes.

Soccer boots are usually made of leather and have light cleats or studs of either rubber, nylon, or light-metal alloys. Heavy metal cleats might injure another player, and so they are not allowed. A player also cannot wear any item such as a ring or watch. The rest of a soccer player's equipment consists of a shirt, shorts, knee-length socks and shin guards. These usually very light guards are the only form of protective padding allowed.

THE BALL

The soccer ball is round and inflated, usually made of leather, and between 27 and 28 inches (68.6 and 71.1 cm) in circumference. In contrast, a basketball is 29 inches (73.7 cm) in circumference, and a volleyball, 26 inches (65 cm). At the start of the game, the soccer ball weighs between 14 and 16 ounces (.40 and .45 kg).

**Controlling a high ball
with the inside of the foot**

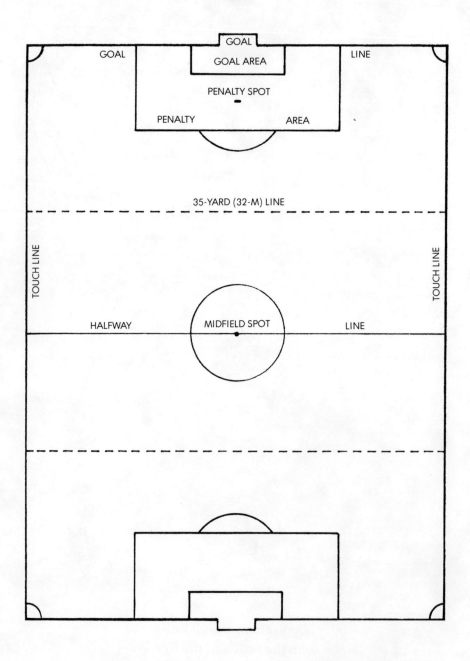

THE FIELD

The overall dimensions of the soccer field are 100 to 130 yards (91.4 to 118.9 m) in length, and 50 to 100 yards (45.7 to 91.4 m) in width. The length of the field must always exceed the width, so that a field of, say, 100 by 100 yards (91.4 by 91.4 m) is not permissible. The field is bounded at the sides by sidelines, or "touchlines," and at the ends, by goal, or "end," lines.

A halfway line running the width of the field divides it into two halves. The middle of this line is the middle of the field of play. It is here that the game begins and is restarted after halftime and after a goal has been scored.

The field in the NASL is different, however. An extra line is drawn across the field 35 yards (32 m) from the goal. Only within that area between the 35-yard (32-m) line and the goal line can a player be off side — instead of in the entire opposing half of the field, as in other countries.

Diagram of Field

THE START

The team captains toss a coin before the start of the game, and the winner may choose either to kick off or to select which end of the field his team will defend in the first half. Of course, if the toss-winning captain chooses to defend an end, then the other team will kick off.

A good captain will note whether wind currents or the glare of the sun may present problems at a particular end. He must remember, too, that the teams change ends at half time and that the sun may be lower and more troublesome then.

Soccer is a simple game, but there are a few technical rules to remember:

A circle with a radius of 10 yards (9.1 m) is drawn around the midfield spot. Only players on the team kicking off may be within that circle at the start and restart of play. This is to insure

**The perfect position for a shot —
the "standing" foot beside the ball,
the "kicking" foot arched so the
instep will make contact with the ball.**

that all opposing players are 10 yards (9.1 m) from the ball when it is about to be kicked.

During the game, play will be restarted from areas other than the midfield spot — such as after a free kick. In those instances, opposing players must also be 10 yards (9.1 m) from the ball. Even though no circles are drawn on the field, except around the midfield spot, it is the player's responsibility — under the eyes of the referee — to make sure that he is at least 10 yards (9.1 m) from the ball at these times.

THE PENALTY AND GOAL AREAS

At each end of the field there is a penalty area, a goal area, and a goal.

The penalty area is a zone 44 yards (40.2 m) wide and 18 yards (16.5 m) out from the goal lines. It is here that much of the hectic action takes place, for most goals are scored from within the penalty area. A good goalkeeper can usually stop a shot that is kicked from farther away.

Certain rules govern the penalty area:

It is only within this area that the goalkeeper may handle the ball. Once he is outside the penalty area, he must follow the same rules as any other player.

It is within this area that the offensive team is awarded a penalty kick. This happens when the defensive team commits a foul. A penalty kick is a free shot at the goal and is made from a "penalty spot" 12 yards (11 m) out from the middle of the goal. It is a straight one-on-one situation, with only the kicker and the goalkeeper allowed within the penalty area. In fact, there is an arc drawn 10 yards (9.1 m) from the penalty spot, and it bulges out beyond the penalty area to make sure that all other players are at

**When a goalkeeper can't catch
the ball, he must punch it away.**

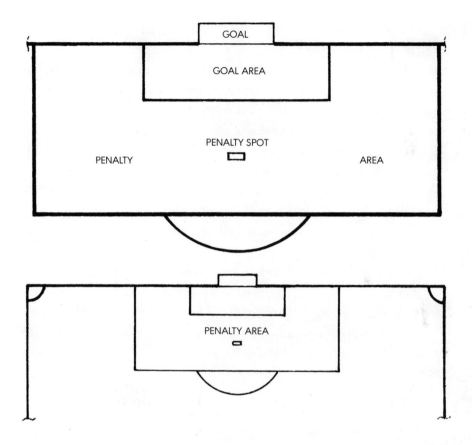

least 10 yards (9.1 m) from the ball when it is kicked. This arc serves the same purpose as the midfield circle.

The goalkeeper cannot move until the penalty kick is made. Since he has an area of 192 square feet (18 sq m) to defend against a ball that is sometimes kicked with a 90-mile-an-hour (145-kmph) force from only 12 yards (11 m) away, it would seem that a penalty kick would never be missed. But it sometimes is.

The goal area is within the penalty area and measures 20 yards (18.3 m) wide by 6 yards (5.5 m) deep. A goalkeeper has special protection within this area. He must not be "charged" — the act of making physical contact with a player — unless he is holding the ball. However, that does not save him from tough collisions when other players are also going for the ball. He can be charged outside the goal area, shoulder to shoulder, if he is holding the ball or obstructing an opponent.

The goalkeeper also takes all his goal kicks from within the goal area. A goal kick is taken when the ball crosses the goal line — outside the goal — and was last touched by a member of the attacking team.

If a member of the defending team last touched it, then the attacking, or offensive, team is given a corner kick. This is taken from the corner of the field closest to the point where the ball went out of play. Usually, the offensive team will have several players clustered around the goal when one of their players kicks the ball hard in from the corner. It can be an exciting, dangerous play.

The goal, which is the final objective of soccer, is an area 8 yards (7.3 m) wide and 8 feet (2.4 m) high. It is marked by two upright posts joined by a crossbar, and these may not be more than 5 inches (12.7 cm) wide. Usually there are nets attached at the back of the goalposts and crossbar. To score a goal, the ball must pass between the posts and under the crossbar.

The whole idea of soccer — all the hard work, skill, artistry, and tough physical tumble — is aimed at getting the ball into the goal.

SCORING

To score a goal, which counts for one point, the whole ball — not just a part of it, as in American football — must pass over the goal line, and between the upright posts and under the crossbar. The ball is not out of play unless all of it crosses the borders of the field. It is in play until the whole ball has crossed either the goal line or the touchline.

The goal does not count if the ball has been thrown, carried, punched, or pushed over the goal line by the hands or arms of a member of the offensive team.

If the ball hits the goalposts and rebounds, if it hits the referee, or even if the player kicking it is off the field of play, it is still in play. If the ball crosses the touchlines, play is restarted by a throw-in — tossing the ball back into play. This is the only time that a player other than the goalkeeper may touch the ball with his hands.

The ball must be thrown in with both hands, from over the thrower's head. The thrower must keep both feet on the ground while throwing. The throw-in is taken by the player of the team opposite to that of the player who last touched the ball.

OFFSIDE

Besides the technical laws of soccer dealt with above, there is one other complicated rule. It covers the position of offside, and is the only law in soccer that restricts the area where a player may go.

A player is off side at the moment the ball is passed to him by a member of his own team and there are not at least two opponents between him and his opponents' goal line. This rule prevents offensive players from staying upfield and waiting for the ball.

However, a player is not off side under the following conditions:

1. When he is in his own half of the field (or, in the NASL, when he is not in the 35-yd. [32-m] offside zone).

2. When he is behind the ball — that is, nearer his own half of the field — when the ball is last touched by a member of his team.

Balance and concentration
are needed to control
the ball on the volley.

3. When the ball is last touched by an opponent.
4. When, at the moment that the player receives the ball from a member of his team, there are two or more opponents between him and their goal line.
5. When he receives a throw-in or corner kick.

It is important to remember that the referee or linesman calls a player on side or off side only at the moment when the ball is *passed* to him, not at the moment when he *receives* it.

After the ball has been kicked or headed toward a player and received by him, he may run where he likes without fear of being off side.

THE REFEREE

The rules of soccer are enforced by a referee, who is in sole command of the game. He is assisted by two officials, called "linesmen."

The referee usually wears a black shirt, black shorts, knee-length socks, and boots. (In North America he sometimes wears a black-and-white-striped shirt.) He also wears two watches, for he is the official timekeeper. In addition, he carries a whistle to signal all his decisions.

The linesmen, each equipped with a bright flag, patrol just outside the touchlines. They use a diagonal system, each one watching over a separate half of the field. The linesmen judge whether or not a ball has gone out of play, and keep in line with the most advanced player of the offensive team so that they can judge an offside. When they see a foul or infringement, they wave their flags. Their actions, however, are not a decision. The linesmen only indicate to the referee that something has happened. The decision is made solely by the referee.

The referee has a difficult job, and it is not made easier by players who argue or protest against his decisions.

THE TEAM

A soccer team consists of eleven players — one goalkeeper and ten outfield players.

Originally, the positions were described as follows:

Goalkeeper	Outside right
Right back	Inside right
Left back	Center forward
Right half	Inside left
Center half	Outside left
Left half	

Basically, the goalkeeper, the two backs, and the center half used to be mainly defensive players.

The two halfbacks — the right half and the left half — plus the inside right and the inside left were the "linking players." They helped out the defensive unit and then took the ball forward for offensive action.

The other three forwards — the outside right, outside left, and center forward — were mainly offensive players. They were the goalscorers.

However, tactics have changed dramatically over the past ten to fifteen years (as will be explained in more detail later), and so positions have been renamed to fit more properly into the modern game.

A listing of player positions would now read:

Goalkeeper	Center midfield
Right back	Left midfield
Center back	Right winger
Center back	Center forward
Left back	Left winger
Right midfield	

However, being assigned to these positions does not mean that the players concern themselves only with their basic jobs. Soccer is a team game that demands a high degree of interplay between members. It also demands a high degree of initiative by the players who are to put into action the tactics set by the coach. So, backs often score goals and forwards often come back to help out hard-pressed defensive units.

A good soccer player is always thinking of ways to help a teammate. He moves into a position where it is easy for his teammate to see him and pass the ball to him.

SUBSTITUTES

Until a few years ago, no substitutions were allowed in soccer. If a player was injured and had to leave the field, his team had to continue with ten men, or nine, or sometimes even with less.

Some countries then began to experiment with various forms of substitution, and in 1967, the FIFA allowed a team to nominate up to five substitutes per game and actually to use up to two of

them. In the NASL, three are permitted to play. Once a substitute replaces a player, that player may not return to the game.

There is only one occasion when a team must play with fewer than eleven players. If a referee sends a player off the field for disciplinary reasons, the player may not return and he may not be replaced. This is one reason why it is so important to play fair and to keep one's temper in soccer. Disciplinary action can leave a team with ten players to face eleven opponents.

Top: although harassed by a defender, this forward watches the ball closely as he prepares to trap it with the inside of his right foot. Bottom: this defender is perfectly balanced as he stretches for a long defensive clearance.

TACTICS

As mentioned earlier, the names (and responsibilities) of the positions on a soccer field have changed a great deal in the past few years. The formation used to be a basic 2–3–5: two backs, three halfbacks, and five forwards. The backs were expected to be big and strong and never to leave their defensive positions. The halfbacks worked in the middle of the field, and the five forwards were expected to remain on the offensive at all times.

But modern ideas have changed the game so that a greater degree of mobility is needed, and new tactics have been introduced.

The two most popular tactical systems in soccer today are the 4–2–4 and the 4–3–3. (Note that the goalkeeper is not included in discussing team formations. No matter what the tactics, his duties are only those of a goalkeeper.)

THE 4–2–4 FORMATION
In the 4–2–4 formation, the team has a line of four backs, two midfield players, and four forwards.

The advantage of this system — which Brazil used in order

to win the 1958 World Cup — is that the two midfield men can move quickly to provide either a six-man defensive action or a six-man offensive action, whichever is needed at a given moment. The system also forces players to think more quickly, because when the two midfield players drop back into defensive action, some of the forwards must slot back into midfield to keep open the lines of communication between the various members of the team. Thus the team moves forward or back as one unit.

A defender might find that the best way he can help one of his teammates is to go forward on a run that takes him up with his own forwards. A forward might spot danger and come sprinting back to strengthen his own defensive action. They each have their own basic job to do, but every player is a member of the team.

THE 4–3–3 FORMATION

The 4–3–3 formation is a variant of the 4–2–4, the change being that one forward is taken back into midfield. This puts the emphasis slightly on defensive soccer. It gives the three midfield players the chance to drop back to make a seven-man defensive unit or go forward into a six-man offensive unit.

This system gives greater offensive opportunities to defenders. Under some of the older systems, there were too many players in front of a back for him ever to find room to run forward and go on to attack. But with a 4–3–3 lineup, the right or left backs often have a great deal of open space in front of them and can run forward to receive the ball and attack.

As we saw earlier, the use of such new tactical systems as the 4–2–4 and 4–3–3 has required changes in the roles, and in the names, of the traditional positions.

Tactics should be chosen to suit the abilities of the players; no player should ever be forced into unsuitable tactics.

The basic point of any tactics is knowing the right moment to pass the ball. The "space" is where the ball is passed. And if the teamwork is right, a teammate will be moving into the right space at just the right time for the ball to be passed.

THE GOALKEEPER

The goalkeeper is a man alone on a soccer field. It is likely that every time he makes a mistake he gives away a goal. So the goalkeeper must keep in mind that the safety of his goal is his first consideration.

It may look good to dive acrobatically, but it is better for his team if the goalkeeper thinks ahead and positions himself so that he does not have to dive.

The goalkeeper must remember these five rules:

1. Always move to meet the ball.
2. Always use both hands to catch or punch the ball away.
3. Always get your body behind the ball whenever possible.
4. When diving at a forward's feet to block the ball, always dive across his feet and not straight at them. (This protects more of the goal and also helps to prevent head injuries.)
5. Throw or kick the ball intelligently to a teammate. Don't kick it aimlessly.

Despite the fact that the goalkeeper stands around more than his ten teammates, he must still be very fit. He should concentrate on exercises to quicken his reactions and strengthen his hands,

arms, and shoulders. One simple exercise is to have two team-mates standing about ten yards (9.1 m) from the goal, throwing or kicking soccer balls to him in rapid succession, changing the height and angle every time they throw or shoot.

A goalkeeper cannot consider the goal area as *his* area. The best goalkeeper is one who is in charge of the entire penalty area, running out from his goal line to meet the ball, catching it in the air, or diving to the ground to stop an opponent from shooting.

Top: protecting the goal — chest behind the shot and both hands ready to catch hold firmly. Bottom: the right way to hold on to a low shot.

DEFENSIVE ACTION

Each player on the team is a defender. And it is important that each player remembers that when the opponents have the ball, everyone on the team is defending, just as every team member is ready to go on the offensive when they themselves have the ball.

This does not mean that each player should turn and start to run back into his own defensive area. Forwards can start their own team's defensive action in their opponents' half of the field. They can do so by "marking" — closely watching — an opposing midfield player so that he is not free to receive a pass. Or they can chase a player for five or ten yards (4.6 or 9.1 m), after he has just intercepted a pass or taken the ball away from another forward.

A forward who loses the ball and then stands still waiting for someone else to give it to him again is a poor forward.

For all real defenders — that is, the backs — the golden rule is "safety first." A defender's mistake is not quite as bad as a goalkeeper's mistake — after all, there is still the goalkeeper to beat. But a mistake near the goal gives a team very little time to recover. It is wise to get the ball quickly away from your goal and cut out the frills. If there is time to think and look, then the ball should be passed accurately and intelligently.

DEFENDING A ZONE

In defending a zone, each player has a roughly defined area to cover, and any opponent coming into that area with the ball is his responsibility.

This is a good defensive system for beginning players to learn, because it teaches one of the most basic rules of soccer — the importance of correct positioning.

DEFENDING "MAN-FOR-MAN"

Each defender has the task of covering one opposing forward. He guards that man wherever he moves, tries to stop him from getting the ball, or tackles him to get the ball away from him if he does receive it. (Tackling is discussed later.)

In theory, this defensive action is perfect because no matter where the enemy forward moves, he is always covered. But this is one of the many theories that do not always work out in practice.

If one member of the defensive unit is beaten, another defender must leave his own man to tackle the onrushing forward. This leaves someone unguarded, so that if the opponents have one really good forward, they will soon find a hole in the defensive unit.

COVERING

A player should always be ready to cover up for any other defender teammate who may be in trouble. For instance, when the play is on the other side of the field from the right back, he should move in from the touchlines and back slightly to cover the center half. Then if the ball is kicked into the middle of the field, he can be close at hand in case of danger.

The greatest danger lies around the edges and inside the penalty area. Very few goals are scored from well outside the penalty area, so a player should be particularly alert whenever he is forced back into the penalty area.

It is also important constantly to be aware of the goalkeeper's activities. When a player is watching the ball, it is easy for him to get in the way of the goalkeeper, who has to run out to catch or punch the ball. Therefore, it is good to have the goalkeeper shout when he is going to run out for the ball, and it is important for other players to listen to what he is shouting.

GETTING POSSESSION OF THE BALL

In soccer, there are three ways of getting possession of the ball — *interception*, the *shoulder charge*, and the *tackle*.

Interception is cutting off a pass before it reaches another opponent. To be successful, the interceptor must be alert and able to move quickly to the ball. Short sprints in training can increase running speed over the first 5 yards (4.6 m).

The shoulder charge is a contact between a player's shoulder and his opponent's shoulder. If the player's arm is not close against his side, then he is nudging his opponent, and this is a foul. If he charges the opponent's back, that is also a foul. The contact must be shoulder to shoulder.

Although the term "tackling" applies to American football, tackling in soccer is not the same action as in football. The soccer

Top: using the body as a shield against an opponent. Bottom: when you must get the ball, tackle hard and go in strong.

tackle is done only with the feet. The player goes in to take the ball away from an opponent — either from the front or in a sliding tackle from the side, much like sliding into base in baseball. A player can go in as hard and as fast as he likes, but he must kick at the ball and not at the opponent. However, players will often come into hard contact with each other at the moment they are both kicking at the ball.

The best time to tackle is at the moment when your opponent is beginning to control the ball, before he can do what he likes with it, and before he starts running with it. If he has full control and a player rushes at him, he has only to turn the ball to one side. The onrushing player is thus beaten, and the opponent runs past him.

When an opponent has control of the ball, the best thing to do is to move to within 2 yards (1.8 m) of him, well-balanced on both feet and ready to lunge at the ball the moment he makes a move. If the tackler is toward one touchline, he can force his opponent away from the goal and out to the less dangerous areas in the wings. He does this by "showing" the opponent the way, that is, by turning his body slightly sideways so that he is blocking the part of the field toward the goal and leaving more open the way toward the touchlines. Then the forward with the ball is more likely to run the way the tackler wants him to run.

OFFENSIVE PLAY

The whole idea of the game is to get the ball into the back of the net. All the attractive play is wasted unless offensive players are able to score. Forwards must be able to shoot quickly, accurately, and with power. Therefore, it is important to have lots of practice at shooting the ball from all angles and from all heights.

A soccer ball will not stand still to allow a player an easy shot. It may be 2 yards (1.8 m) in the air in front of him or bouncing awkwardly at his side. It may be coming toward him from a defender's clearance or it may be running away from him after a pass from one of his teammates behind him.

And he may have only a second to get in his shot.

At practice, a soccer player should set up situations that cover all kinds of shots, not just the easy ones. He may miss more than he scores, but even the great players miss many a goal. The professionals just forget about it and keep alert for the next chance. It is better to try a difficult shot at the goal and miss than not to try it at all.

Soccer teams have different offensive formations and play patterns that they try to follow. Each team should choose formations to suit the players on that particular team.

The inside-of-the-foot pass

For instance, if all the forwards in a club are small, quick players, the object should be to pass accurately, rapidly, and close to the ground, and so use the speed and skill of such players.

If a team has a big burly center forward, his ability to make hard passes in the middle of the field can be applied in two ways.

First, he can be used as a "wall," by bouncing the ball off him to get past an opponent. His team member hits the ball hard at him and keeps running. The "wall" turns the ball sideways. The defender who has gone in to challenge him is left stranded. Then the team member regains the ball and goes on to shoot.

The second way of using the center forward's height and strength is by sending high passes into the goal area, where he can head at the goal.

HEADING

Many people ask, "Doesn't a soccer ball hurt when you head it?" The answer is a definite no, as long as two simple rules are followed.

The first essential rule for heading requires that the soccer player keeps his eyes on the ball at all times. His natural reflex action is to close his eyes as the ball comes toward him. But by constant practice he will learn to keep them open until the actual split second of contact. The correct part of the head to use is the forehead. The flatness of the forehead enables the player to be accurate in directing the ball.

The second basic rule in heading is equally important. A soccer player must never let the ball hit him — he must hit the ball. This means that as the ball comes toward him, he must tense his neck muscles and hit at the ball with his forehead, and not just stand still and let the ball hit him.

When a player is learning to head the ball, it is better to use a soft soccer ball or, better still, a plastic ball until he begins to gain confidence. A good simple practice to start with is to throw a ball 2 feet (.6 m) above the head and, as it falls, head it back into the air, trying each time to head it higher. More height can be obtained by pushing the head and neck forward to meet the ball. Bracing the neck muscles gives more power. This is only practice to help in gaining confidence; in a real game, no player has to head the ball straight into the air.

Once a player has confidence, it is important for him to learn to jump for a ball and head it in any direction. If he stands still with both feet on the ground and waits for the ball, he will have beaten himself. Against a good opponent, he will never touch the ball because his opponent will simply jump above him and head the ball away.

For a player to be good "in the air," the timing of his jump is vital and needs a great deal of practice. Use a short run and jump up from one foot. This gives greater height than a standard jump using both feet. It is a common fault to watch an opponent who is also trying to head the ball, instead of watching the ball.

So, remember the first basic rule — *never take your eye off the ball.*

**Following the rules
for heading the ball**

THE FOULS

The nine worst fouls in soccer, called the "penal fouls," are:

Holding an opponent.
Striking or attempting to strike an opponent.
Pushing an opponent.
Handling the ball.
Kicking or attempting to kick an opponent.
Jumping at an opponent.
Tripping an opponent.
Charging an opponent in a violent or dangerous manner.
Charging an opponent from behind (unless he is intentionally obstructing).

For any of these infractions, a direct free kick is given to the other team. A direct free kick is a kick that is taken from the point where the foul occurred, and no player on the offending team is

**Getting ready for a
long kick, left foot landing
by the side of the ball.**

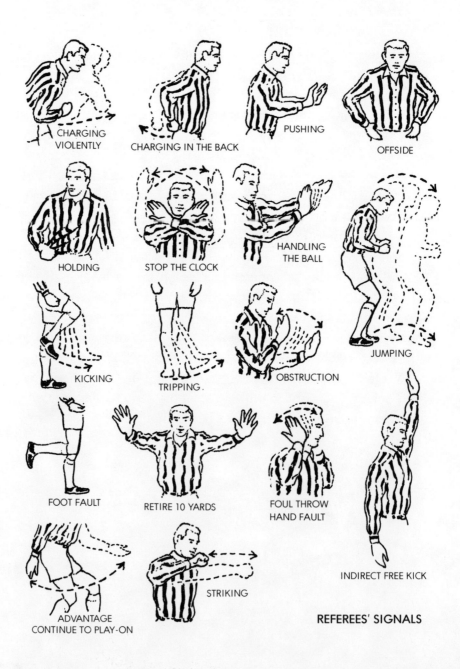

REFEREES' SIGNALS

allowed within 10 yards (9.1 m) of the kicker. A goal can be scored directly from the kick if the kick is within range of the goal.

There are also lesser technical infringements. They include obstruction, that is, intentionally getting in the way of an opponent when not trying to play the ball; touching the ball more than once when kicking off or taking a free kick or corner kick; and throwing in the ball to oneself. (After all situations in which the ball is "dead," the player must kick or throw the ball to another player before the player can touch it again himself.)

A player also commits an infringement if he uses unmannerly language with game officials or with other players.

For these lesser infringements, the opposing team is given indirect free kicks. The ball cannot be shot directly into the goal but must be touched by at least one other player first. Like the direct free kick, an indirect free kick is taken from the point where the foul occurred.

A referee will signal that he is giving an indirect free kick by raising one arm straight in the air above his head. Unless the referee gives this signal, the free kick is assumed to be a direct free kick.

FITNESS

Both skill and hard work are necessary to play soccer well, but you can neither work hard nor be skillful unless you are really fit. Soccer requires a greater degree of physical fitness than almost any other sport.

A soccer player's whole body must be in good shape. Certainly, he uses his legs most of all, but his entire body must be in trim to endure all the leaping, jumping, and hard physical challenge that are required in the game of soccer.

At the start of the season, players can begin their physical training by cross-country running and "lapping" the soccer field — alternate sprinting, jogging, and walking around and around the soccer field. They should do the standard gymnastic exercises with regularity and work up gradually to the highest possible peak of fitness.

**Physical fitness and
endurance are all-important.**

The most important training in soccer is working in situations that resemble an actual match. This is true for any sport. A 100-yard (91.4-m) sprinter does not run a marathon race in training; he sprints and sprints and sprints. A weight lifter need not run at all. And so, a soccer player needs to train under the conditions that he will meet during the 90 minutes of a soccer match.

Five-a-side soccer outdoors and "box soccer" indoors — which is a five- or six-a-side game in a gymnasium — are both of great value in making players exert themselves in controlling a soccer ball and passing it as they would in an actual game. It is much better to work at shooting, for instance, when being challenged, than when the ball is not in motion and no one is trying to stop you. This would never happen in an actual game.

Gradually, as fitness and skill increase, players could take part in full-scale matches, where they might be given certain handicaps to increase their ability. For instance, for a part of the match, they might be told that every time the ball comes to them, they could only touch it three times: to control the ball, to make sure it is well-placed, and to pass it. Then they might be told to touch it only twice — "control" and "pass." Or, they might have to beat an opponent while running with the ball before passing. Sometimes they might be allowed to use only the right foot or only the left.

Finally, the coach might insist that they play one-touch soccer — that is, they must pass the ball immediately as it comes to them. To do this accurately requires the highest degree of technique. Even at the top professional level, one-touch soccer is enormously demanding.

Continual practice will overcome setbacks and is the sure way to improvement.

LAST WORDS

Always remember that soccer is a team game. It is not just two separate units, defensive and attacking.

All top-class teams throughout the world are hardworking units, and each player is prepared to give his utmost to the game. If his team is forced on the defensive, a forward must be ready to turn and run back quickly to help the defenders, or be in position to receive a pass when possession of the ball is regained. When his team goes on the offensive, a defender must move up quickly in support of his forwards, so that at all times the team is a single, united force.

GREAT NAMES IN SOCCER

These are some of the outstanding countries, teams, players, and managers that are known to soccer fans the world over.

Argentina: one of the strongest of the South American soccer nations. Estudiantes, Independiente and Racing Club are three of its best teams. Argentina was winner and host country for the 1978 World Cup.

Banks, Gordon: goalkeeper on England's 1966 World Cup Championship team. Later he lost the sight of one eye but played superbly for Fort Lauderdale Strikers of the NASL, which he joined in 1977. Although less spectacular than many goalkeepers, he has the two great essentials — perfect sense of positioning and perfect sense of timing.

Beckenbauer, Franz: dominant captain of F.C. Bayern, Munich, three times champion of Europe, and of West Germany's 1974 World Cup winning team until he signed for the Cosmos of New York in 1977.

Best, George: flamboyant winger of Northern Ireland and Manchester United, as famous for his escapades as for his soccer until traded to the Los Angeles Aztecs. There he became, naturally, one of the NASL's great attractions.

Bradley, Gordon: played for, coached, and directed the Cosmos, molding them from a fledgling club into one of the world's most famous teams. He is now vice president and head coach of the Washington Diplomats.

Brazil: World Cup champion in 1958, 1962, and 1970, and a country with almost limitless talent — as well as the biggest stadium in the world, the 200,000-seat Maracana, in Rio de Janeiro.

Cruyff, Johann: captain of Holland's national team, Ajax of Amsterdam, who led his club to three European titles before signing a series of million-dollar contracts with Barcelona of Spain.

Di Stefano, Alfredo: legendary center forward of Real ("ray-ahl") Madrid, and one of the world's most notable all-around soccer players until his retirement in 1966.

England: World Cup champion in 1966 and one of the greatest soccer nations since 1863.

Eusebio: known as the "Black Panther," is one of the greatest goal-scorers of all time. His full name is Eusebio da Silva Ferreira. Born in Mozambique, Eusebio played for the Benfica club in Portugal. Later he played for Toronto and Las Vegas in the NASL.

Fontaine, Juste: the Frenchman who holds the world record for goal scoring in a World Cup tournament. He scored thirteen goals in six games in the 1958 tournament in Sweden.

Gaetjens, Joe: scored the most famous goal in United States soccer history — the point that beat England in the 1950 World Cup in Belo Horizonte, Brazil. Gaetjens was born in Haiti and later became an American citizen.

Garrincha: one of the most spectacular players in the sport, who was an amazing outside right for Brazil. His real name is Manoel dos Santos; his nickname, Garrincha, means "Little Bird."

Hungary: produced a revolution in soccer tactics in the early 1950s and became the first nation ever to beat England on British home ground. The great Hungarian team was nicknamed the "Magical Magyars."

Hurst, Geoff: scored three goals for England in the World Cup final against West Germany, the only player to accomplish such a feat. Hurst played for West Ham United of London and later for the Seattle Sounders of the NASL.

Italy: one of Europe's superior soccer nations, with the wealthiest clubs — Internazionale, A.C. Milan, Juventus, Torino, and A.S. Roma — all capable of spending $1 million on a player they want. Italy won the World Cup in 1934 and 1938.

McAllister, Jimmy: typical of the scores of young American players now becoming good professionals. He plays for the Seattle Sounders and was the recipient of Pele's game shirt after the 1977 NASL Soccer Bowl — a symbolic handing over of the game of soccer from the veteran Pele to the rookie McAllister.

Mexico: host for the 1970 World Cup finals, and the nation that boasts the player with the most remarkable record for international soccer: Goalkeeper Antonio Carbajal played in five World Cup finals — in 1950, 1954, 1958, 1962, and 1966 — and in the Olympic Games in 1948.

Muller, Gerd: called "Der Bomber" by his fans because of the hundreds of goals he has scored for his club, Bayern Munich, and for West Germany.

Pele: called the world's greatest — and probably the highest-paid soccer player of all time. The real name of this brilliant Brazilian forward is Edson Arantes do Nascimento. In 1958, at the age of seventeen, he played for Brazil in the World Cup finals. He retired from the Cosmos in 1977.

Puskas, Ferenc: a former major in the Hungarian army, and the greatest player in Hungarian history. After the Hungarian uprising in 1956, he became a refugee and found sanctuary in Spain, where he starred for Real Madrid. In 1968, he was appointed the coach of the Vancouver Royals in the North American Soccer League and later coached around the world.

Ramsey, Sir Alfred: played right back for England. As a manager, Ramsey led England to victory in the 1966 World Cup. Born a commoner, he was knighted by Queen Elizabeth II for his efforts.

Real Madrid: six-time champion of Europe. This Madrid club is one of the finest ever to play soccer. No other team has been champion of Europe so often, and hardly any other club ever wins the championship of Spain.

Rous, Sir Stanley: honorary President of FIFA, and former secretary of the English Football Association.

Roy, Willie: one of the top goal scorers during the first year of professional soccer in the United States. This Chicagoan is now director of development for the Chicago Sting.

Santos: the world champion club from the coffee port of Brazil that brought the peerless Pele to the world.

Scotland: home of thousands of great soccer players and two great teams — Glasgow Celtic and Glasgow Rangers — which between them have won almost every Scottish championship in the twentieth century.

Spain: a nation which, although known as "a nation of matadors," boasts more soccer fans than bullfighting enthusiasts. Spain will be host of the 1982 World Cup finals— the year the U.S. expects to have built a young team capable of qualifying for the last sixteen competing nations.

Uruguay: World Cup winner in 1930 and 1950.

U.S.S.R.: a giant in soccer, playing the most disciplined, regimented soccer in the world. Moscow Dynamo, Moscow Torpedo, and Kiev Dynamo are the three most famous teams.

West Germany: world champion in 1954 and 1974. This nation produces some of the most dynamic soccer players in the world.

Wilson, Bruce: born in Vancouver, a left back who is commonly regarded as the best player North America has produced.

Yachin, Lev: the Russian goalkeeper who was one of the world's finest for some twenty years. He stands six feet four inches (1.9 m) tall, and has massive hands and fantastic reflexes. His club is Moscow Dynamo.

GLOSSARY OF SOCCER TERMS

Center — the act of kicking the ball from either flank into the goal-mouth, the "center of danger." "To cross" the ball is the same as "to center" the ball.

Charge — the act of making hard physical contact with another player by fair means.

Corner — short for "corner kick," the kick awarded to the offensive team at the place where the touchlines and goal lines meet. It occurs when a member of the defensive team plays the ball over his own goal line.

CSA — the Canadian Soccer Association, the governing body of Canadian soccer.

Draw — same as a tie; the scores are even.

Dribble — to run with the ball under control at the feet.

Drop Ball — a ball dropped into play by the referee, at the point where play stopped, after any unusual halt in the game (such as for an injury to a player).

EFA — the English Football Association, the governing body of English soccer.

End Line — see *goal line.*

Field — the playing area, between 100 and 130 yards (91.4 m, 118.9 m) long and between 50 and 100 yards (45.7 m, 91.4 m) wide.

FIFA — Fédération Internationale de Football Association, the world governing body of soccer.

Foul — any act contrary to the Laws of the Game.

Four-Three-Three (4–3–3) — a system of play that uses a line of four defenders, three midfield players, and three forwards.

Four-Two-Four (4–2–4) — a system of play that uses, in front of a goalkeeper, a line of four defenders, two midfield players, and four offensive forwards.

Free Kick — a kick awarded when a member of the opposing team commits a foul. The ball is placed on the spot where the foul occurred and a player has a free kick at it.

Free Kick, Direct — awarded for the more serious fouls. It may be shot directly into the goal.

Free Kick, Indirect — awarded for lesser fouls. It must be touched by the kicker and at least one other player before a goal can be scored.

Goal Area — the zone, 6 yards (5.5 m) by 20 yards (18.3 m), inside each penalty area in front of each goal.

Goal Kick — the kick taken by the goalkeeper to restart play when his opponents have put the ball over the goal line — outside the goal.

Goal Line — the line drawn at each end of the field of play. Also called "end line."

Goal Nets — the nets draped from the goalposts to stop the ball when a goal has been scored. They must be fixed tightly to the goalposts so that the ball cannot squeeze through.

Goalposts — the two uprights — 8 feet (2.4 m) high — and one crossbar — 8 yards (7.3 m) long — that make up the goal at each end of the field.

Halfway Line — the line drawn across the middle of the field to divide it into halves.

Hands — the foul committed when a player other than the goalkeeper touches the ball with his hands or arms on the field of play.

Hat Trick — three goals scored by one player in succession in the same match.

Heading — using the head to move the ball. "Header" describes a player who excels at heading ("He is a good header").

International — the title given to a player who has played for his nation's all-star team against foreign opposition.

Kickoff — the kick from a spot in the middle of the field which starts the game and restarts it at half time and after each goal.

Linesmen — the two officials who assist the referee. They remain off the field of play on the touchlines.

Marking — closely watching an opponent so that he can be challenged for the ball as soon as he receives it.

Offside — occurs if the ball is passed to a player by a member of his own team, the player being in the opponents' half of the field with fewer than two opponents between him and the opponent's goal. In the case of the NASL, offside is only possible in the 35-yard (32-m) offside zone.

Own Goal — when a player accidentally puts the ball into his own goal. The score is counted for the other team, and the man who made the mistake is "credited" with scoring an own goal.

Pass — the movement of the ball from one player to another.

Penalty Area — the zone, 18 yards (16.5 m) by 44 yards (40.2 m), in front of each goal.

Penalty Kick — a kick at the goal, taken from a point 12 yards (11 m) from the middle of the goal (penalty spot) when the defending team has committed a foul inside the penalty area.

Referee — the official in sole charge of the game, assisted by two linesmen.

Save — a shot, or header, that a goalkeeper stops from going into the goal.

Shin Guards — the only protective padding in soccer. They are light, thin pads made of foam rubber or similar material.

Shot — the kick at the goal made with the aim of scoring a goal.

Sidelines — see *touchlines*.

Tackle — the act of trying to take the ball away from another player.

Throw-in — when the ball goes over the touchlines and is thrown back into play by a member of the team that did not touch it last.

Touchlines — the lines drawn at each side of the field. Also called sidelines.

Trap — controlling the ball with the foot, chest, or thigh.

U.S.S.F. — United States Soccer Federation, the governing body of U.S. soccer.

Winger — the offensive player on either flank of the attack, right winger or left winger. Also called outside right, outside left.

Wing Half — the player on either flank in midfield who does either offensive or defensive jobs.

World Cup — the championship for national all-star teams. The eliminations take two years, and the finals are played in a different country every four years.

INDEX

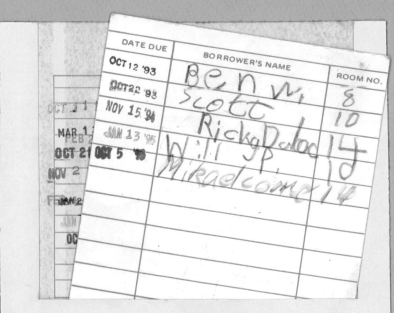

DATE DUE	BORROWER'S NAME	ROOM NO.
OCT 12 '93	Ben W.	8
OCT 22 '93	Scott	
NOV 15 '94	RickgDaloc	10
JAN 13 '95		14
OCT 5 '95	Will g.B.	10
	Miraelcome	14

796.33
T

Toye, Clive

Soccer.